Whimsical
ANIMALS
COLORING BOOK

ILLUSTRATED BY KERRIE HUBBARD

Animals are such agreeable friends-
they ask no questions,
they pass no criticisms.

-George Eliot

For more information please visit:
www.kerriehubbard.com

ISBN: 9798644566280

To Carol,
who in the face of massive adversity,
continues keep a smile on her face
and hope in her heart.

COLORED BY:

____

DATE STARTED:

____

DATE FINISHED:

____

Don't Worry, Bee Happy

HAPPY

Chloe decided to see if she could
have her luck and eat it too.

It is nice to think how easily one can
be hidden in a field of daisies.

Meadow never liked surprises.
Even on her birthday.

Darren could never pass up a dare, but wished he would have paid more attention during swimming lessons as a kid.

YOU FLOAT MY GOAT

And just like that,
Sally's world turned upside down

Stan knew it sounded like a cliche'
but he blurted it out anyway:
'Naomi, Llama gonna love you forever'.

The moment Delores realized her mother
was not an appreciator of the arts.

Mother
Hen

Love is blind.
Or maybe just a bit cross-eyed.

LOVE
xoxo
XOXO
xoxo
LOVE
LOVE
LOVE
LOVE
XOXO
XXOO
XXOO
XOXO
LOVE

Tiptoeing through the tulips
proved to be harder than Cal anticipated.

Harry got his motor running
and took off down the highway...

He had a feeling he was
born to be wild.

There's no bunny like
Snow Bunny

Now and then we had a hope
that if we lived and were good,
God would permit us to be pirates.
-Mark Twain

Dottie took the term 'Party Animal'
to a new extreme.

HAPPY CAT
TREATS
HAPPY MEOW
OF MICE AND CATS

The early bird gets the tea
(and the peace and quiet).

RISE & SHINE

You've got a friend in me.
-Woody

Just one more chapter...

WelcOME
LITTLE HOUSE IN THE BIG FOREST

Lois decided to take matters into her own hands and create her own happiness.

Marvin dreamed of visiting the 'all-you-can-eat' buffet for at least half of his nine lives. But now that he was here, just the thought of it made him a bit queasy.

Allen resigned himself to the fact that he was the night owl of the family.

Coloring Cards

The following pages contain the original 20 full-page images in 4x6 card size. Color them up, cut them out and send them to someone you care about.

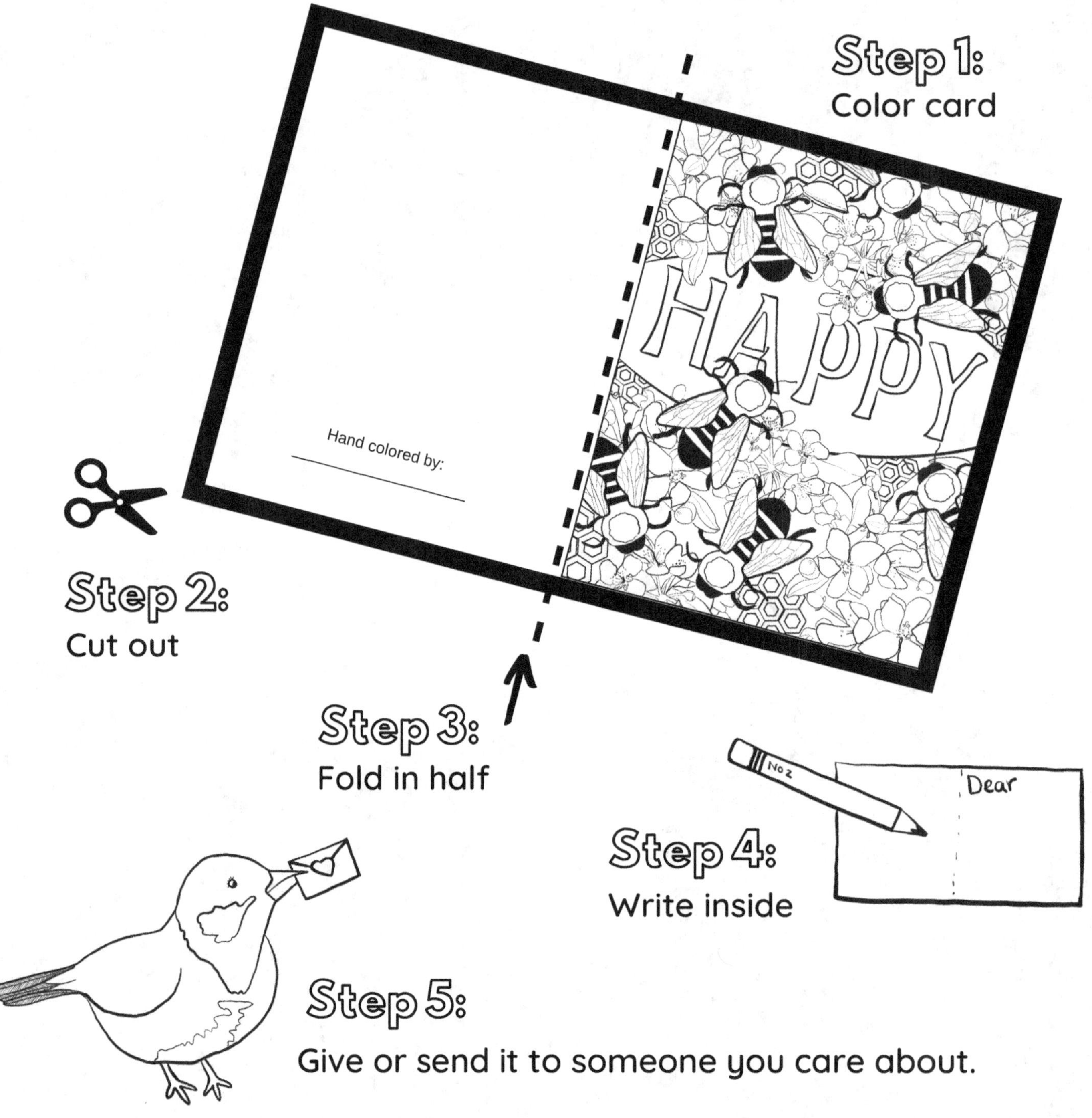

Hand colored by:

____

©Kerrie Hubbard KerrieHubbard.com

Hand colored by:

____

©Kerrie Hubbard KerrieHubbard.com

Hand colored by:

____

Hand colored by:

____

Hand colored by:

____

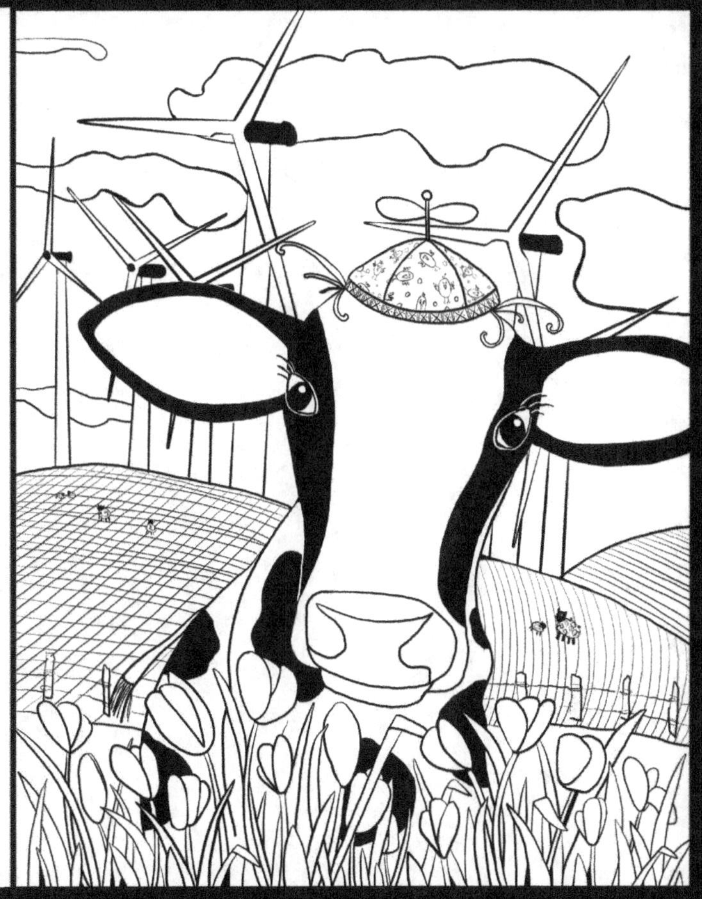

Hand colored by:

____

Hand colored by:

____

©Kerrie Hubbard ❀ KerrieHubbard.com

Hand colored by:

____

©Kerrie Hubbard ❀ KerrieHubbard.com

Hand colored by:

____

©Kerrie Hubbard ✿ KerrieHubbard.com

Hand colored by:

____

©Kerrie Hubbard ✿ KerrieHubbard.com

Hand colored by:

____

Hand colored by:

____

Hand colored by:

____

Hand colored by:

____

Hand colored by:

____

©Kerrie Hubbard ❀ KerrieHubbard.com

Hand colored by:

____

©Kerrie Hubbard ❀ KerrieHubbard.com

Hand colored by:

____

© Kerrie Hubbard   KerrieHubbard.com

Hand colored by:

____

© Kerrie Hubbard   KerrieHubbard.com

Hand colored by:

____

©Kerrie Hubbard ✿ KerrieHubbard.com

Hand colored by:

____

©Kerrie Hubbard ✿ KerrieHubbard.com

You made it to the end! Hurrah!
I hope you had fun coloring the pages in this book.
If so, could you please do me a favor and leave a review on Amazon?
It helps me be found by others who might also enjoy coloring these images.
Thanks! I super appreciate it!

For more of my coloring books, journals and notebooks, check out my website:

KERRIEHUBBARD.com

Thanks for coloring with me!

KERRIE HUBBARD *Studio*

www.ingramcontent.com/pod-product-compliance
Lightning Source LLC
Chambersburg PA
CBHW081319250726

48662CB00008B/2655